Know Your Mind

H. H. Sri Sri Ravi Shankar

Know Your Mind

1st edition: September 2011

Printed in India by Jwalamukhi Mudranalaya Pvt. Ltd., Bangalore
Ph: +91-80-26601064, 26617243

ISBN: 978-81921798-1-0

Sri Sri Publications Trust,
Art of Living International Centre,
21st KM, Kanakapura Road, Udayapura, Bangalore - 560082.
Phone: 080-32722473
Email: info@srisripublications.com
Website: store.artofliving.org

CONTENTS

WHEN THE MIND VANISHES

When will there be no questions? Questions will not exist when one has no intelligence or when the mind is at peace. That is a good thing. Isn't it? An excellent state!

It is impossible not to have any intelligence at all. Everybody has at least a little bit of intelligence. When you cross over intelligence and the mind gets into feelings and innocence, then no questions will arise. Even if a question arises, that question will be satisfied by small answers itself. Look at children. They ask something like where did this elephant come from and if you say it came from the forest, they just become silent. They agree with you. Isn't it?

All the questions in the mind should be converted to exclamations. That is why they say, "*Yo buddhi paratattva sâ.*" That which is beyond the intellect is the Divine. You will not get the Divine if you attempt to catch the Divine through the intellect.

Thoughts arise, therefore thoughts have a source. If you go on a road, you can only see a small part of the road you cannot see the whole road. But if you are seated in an aircraft, then you can see the beginning and the end of the road from the aircraft. If you are seated in a car, you can only see a few hundred meters of the road. At the most you can see half a kilometer of the road. But from the aircraft you can see the whole road, from the beginning to its end.

In the same way, as our consciousness keeps expanding more and more, you get to know more about the past and the future. All this begins to happen naturally, but none of the happenings are great events in any case!

The important thing is to live in the present moment. The mind always swings between the past and the future. When this swinging stops, then the time stops too. That is our true nature. The mind is like a firefly which gets attracted towards light. The mind, like the firefly, is constantly searching for its source through various objects. When it gets surprised, it begins to search for its source. The moment it obtains the vision of its source, the mind vanishes. This is a technique of meditation.

You must have heard this story. Once, Lord *Krishna* developed a severe headache because there were too many *gopis* and they were constantly fighting about this and that. All this caused him a severe headache. *Radha* was seated near him and was pressing his head. Even that did not help *Krishna*.

Then *Krishna* said, "*Radha*, stand on my head and put the whole weight of your body on my head." *Radha* agreed to this and stood on *Krishna's* head. The other *gopis* who saw this came running to her and said, "Oh! *Radha*! What are you doing? You will go to hell. You are standing on the Lord's head!" Do you know what *Radha* replied?

Radha said, "I am prepared to spend all my life in hell. If my Lord can be relieved of his headache even for two minutes by this act of mine, then that is sufficient for me. I am ready to spend my whole life in hell just for those two minutes."

All of them there appreciated *Radha's* devotion and the depth of her devotion. That was because every cell of *Radha* was dedicated only to *Krishna*. For her there was nothing but *Krishna* in the whole world. She was totally immersed in *Krishna*. *Radha's* love was so complete. Why was *Radha* only the most favourite of *Krishna* amongst all the *gopis*? Why did *Krishna* love *Radha* the most? This the *gopis* understood.

Radha was totally selfless. She had nothing inside her. That is why *Radha* is first and then comes *Govinda* – *Radhe Govinda*! *Radha* would breathe *Krishna*. *Radha* obtained a higher state than *Krishna*. So if you ever wish to worship *Krishna*, then first you need to become *Radha* and then worship *Krishna*.

If you want to worship *Rama*, you should become *Hanuman* first and then worship *Rama*. *Rama* could not have won the war without the help of *Hanuman*. *Rama* required *Hanuman's* help. That is why *Hanuman* is greater than *Rama*.

If you want to be a servant then be a servant like *Hanuman*. If you want to be a lover, then be a lover like *Radha*. If you want to do penance, then do penance like *Parvati*. To perform the worship of *Shiva*, we have to become *Parvati* first and then worship *Shiva*. *Parvati* had only one desire in her, to obtain *Shiva*.

Hanuman is said to have 14 *kalaas* or digits whereas *Rama* had only 12 *kalaas* or digits. *Hanuman* would breathe *Rama*. *Hanuman* is greater than *Rama*. That is why he could carry *Rama* on his shoulders and help him. Isn't it? Who else can help? *Hanuman* became a devotee and therefore much more powerful.

BATHING THE MIND

You wear good clothes and go out. It could be new or neatly ironed. However the cloth may be, you wear it and go out. What happens then? It becomes dirty. Then you have to wash it. Isn't it?

Similarly you bathe and apply scent all over your body. How long will it stay? It will stay for a little while. Then you have to take a bath again the next day. Isn't it? Say, you do not have bath for two or three days, what happens by the third day? Nobody will come near you on the third day. "Oh! I just had my bath the day before yesterday. I have become dirty again. So my bath of the day before yesterday was in vain." If you go on in this manner, then what is there to say! If anybody goes on in this manner you will call them mad.

Our mind is also similar to this. Isn't it? Once you bathe your body, you have to bathe it all over again the next day. Sometimes you may have to bathe that same evening. If it is a very hot summer day, then you may have to bathe two to three times. If it is winter, bathing the next day will be sufficient.

Nobody says that they will only bathe if their body is dirty and greasy. Nobody keeps sniffing themselves and then decide to have a bath. Whether there is a smell or not, whether the body is dirty or clean, we bathe everyday. Isn't it? Similarly nobody will take off their clothes to see whether it is dirty and if it needs washing. We will not wait till the whole cloth is so dirty that the colour of clothes is not at all visible and then only decide to wash the clothes. What do we do even if a little dirt is visible on the cloth? We wash the cloth. But does the dirt belong to us? The dirt is of the cloth isn't it? Dirt is the nature of cloth.

So too, the nature of the body is dirt. Assume that your hand becomes muddy and tar or some colour is stuck to it. Do you then sit crying? Do you cry: "Oh, my hands are all muddy?" No. You immediately go and wash your hands by applying soap. If the dirt is too stubborn and does not go away easily, you continue to scrub and wash it for at least an hour. Then you come away satisfied that your hands are clean.

Suppose your hands are stained with deep colours or charcoal, it takes at least two days for it to go away. But still you continue your efforts without calling it quits, without spoiling the peace of your mind.

So too is the mind. There is always happiness and sadness happening in the mind. In addition to the happiness and sadness which happens to you, others' happiness and sadness also comes and sits on you. Even then it is dirt. Isn't it? You have not dirtied your clothes but an auto rickshaw passed by you during a rainy day and splashed all the dirt of the road onto your clothes and your clothes became dirty. Then what is the use of shouting at the auto rickshaw driver and asking him why he did it. Do we sit still and think that this dirt was caused by somebody and not me? We go ahead and wash the clothes and become clean. Our mind too is very similar.

Happiness and sadness appear in our mind and disappear. Therefore, sit down and meditate for a while, do *pranayama, bhajans* and prayer.

What happens to the mind then? It gets washed and becomes cleaner once again.

You do not have to sit and wait for difficulties or sadness to strike you and then you commence doing all these things. If you keep practising every day then you will not have any problems or difficulties. If something still happens to you, you need not sit and worry, "Oh, this has happened, that has happened." Are you clean? Know this. Is your nature pure? Are you, your nature of permanence and purity?

Then sin will never reach you. It is impossible for your sins to touch you. You have to understand this very well. That is why it is said that just by immersing yourself in water all your sins vanish away. Like bathing and washing away your body dirt, once you immerse your head into water and bathe and all your sins leave you. We also think that our sins go away if we give gifts to somebody. Sin is not our nature.

We usually fill ourselves with a guilty conscience. The feeling of guilt itself pulls us down. When you have this feeling in your mind that 'I am a sinner', then it is not possible to do *sadhana*. What happens because of the feeling of guilt? You get angry. From anger emotions begin to arise. All kinds of impure feelings begin to arise in your mind.

What should be done to free oneself from the feeling of guilt? We have to discover our purity. We do not have to go somewhere in order to get our purity. You should bring this awareness in your mind: 'I am pure'. For this awareness to exist deep inside you, you should increase your *prana shakti* or the life force energy. *Sudarshana Kriya*, meditation, *bhajans, pranayama* and everything else is done to increase the life force. Mind becomes pure and lighter. If some dirt comes and settles down on it and the mind becomes impure again, then what should be done? We should never forget: 'my nature is pure'.

The mind is like a transparent crystal. Whatever colour is placed behind the crystal, the crystal refracts that light. Similarly, the emotions and feelings in the environment like: anger, jealousy, hatred and desires, all get reflected in the mind. When it gets reflected, it is foolish to sit and brood. "Oh, this happened to me. I am like that." You have to keep becoming aware, aware of the truth that 'I am pure. I am ever pure'. This is known as *viveka* or discrimination.

Then *'Shiva tulyo jayate'*

[*Shiva* refers to *Shiva*; *Tulyo* means like and *jayate* means become i.e. you become like *Shiva*. *Shiva Sutras* 3.25]

Then our consciousness becomes like *Shiva*. What is *Shiva*? Pure, transparent light. The consciousness which is as pure as a crystal.

'Shudda vidya pradayakam'

[*Shudda* is pure, *Vidya* is knowledge and *Pradayakam* is giver i.e. the pure give of knowledge].

'Nityam purnam chidanandam'

[*Nityam* means eternal, *purnam* is full and *chidanandam* is one whose consciousness is bliss].

Full. There is no lack of anything whatsoever. If there is a lack, then the feeling of guilt follows it.

'Sadashivam aham bhaje'

[*Sada-shivam* means to the eternal *Shiva*, *aham* is I and *bhaje* is to bow down i.e. I bow down to the eternal *Shiva*].

Understand that our consciousness is knowledge. You yourself are knowledge. There is no need to seek knowledge elsewhere. Whereas, if you feel that the mind is not pure, then you need to do penance in order to purify it.

What is *tapas* or penance? It is a process done for a specific period of time. When the mind becomes impure then fasting for one, two, three, five or seven days and only consuming water or fasting with fruits and water can be done. Penance or *tapas* happens through this. Singing the praise of the lord, *bhajans*, also constitutes *tapas*.

'Nasti samam pranayamam tapam'

(*Nasti* is not present, *samam* means equal to, *pranayamam* is *pranayama* and *tapam* means penance i.e. there is no penance equal to *pranayama*).

It has been said that there is no penance equal to *pranayama*. See, how bored you get when you sit down and do *pranayamas,* but there is no other *tapas* equal to it. There is nothing else which can equal it and purify the mind. This is the one thing.

The other thing is remembering the name of the lord, singing and listening to *satsang,* all equals *tapas.* By doing these the mind becomes pure and clear. This is our true nature.

If the mind gets dirty again you feel bad about it. If you feel bad about it, then the mind becomes further impure. You indulge in self blame by thinking: 'I am less, something is not right'. The feeling of guilt becomes firm.

You should not indulge in self-blame or harbour the feeling of guilt. With the firm conviction in the mind - 'my nature is pure' - you should continue to meditate and do *tapas* everyday.

SPREADING NOBLE THOUGHTS

If we keep discussing noble thoughts with each other, then the mind expands. Our belief and faith deepens. What do we usually do? We keep our experiences to ourselves and do not share them with any body. What happens if we do not share? The mind will not acquire a firm or decisive intellect then. How does our mind and intellect become shaky? We listen to the words uttered by a few people and become shaky. Isn't it? Until the consciousness is firm, what does a person do? "Oh! Everybody goes there? Okay, then I will go too." Usually you will not go where no people go. You think, "Is everybody going? So in that case it is not possible for everybody to be fools. One or two could be fools. Not everybody." Mind tells you to move according to the crowd.

Therefore, in the *satsang*, if each one of you begins sharing all the great experiences you have begun experiencing in your lives and share all the noble thoughts, what happens? Your self confidence and sincerity becomes stronger. You can go forward if you have faith. The more faith you have, the further you can progress. In order to strengthen your belief, you should keep on participating in *satsangs*. You should also keep participating in celebrations. Not just sit in a dull manner. Are you getting this?

Do not differentiate life and *satsang*. So what do we do to work in this direction? Sit in the *satsang* and discuss about life. What happened? How angry your mother-in-law was with you today, how much you screamed at your daughter-in-law, how much you fought at home today... you can talk about all these in the *satsang*. Instead of sitting in front of the courtyard of your house and gossiping, come to *satsang* and gossip. When you gossip in *satsang*, your life blends with knowledge and your whole life gets transformed.

Otherwise, if you sit in *satsang* and speak only *Brahma gyana* (the highest knowledge), and then get back to your routine life and gossip, you will continue to remain only in your gossip and will have no progress in life.

You all conduct your daily meetings across the compound walls or in your courtyard. Isn't it? So in those meetings, for fifteen to twenty minutes at least mix knowledge into your gossip. Then *satsang* begins to happen even in your gossiping sessions. Mix *satsang* in your gossip and gossip in *satsang*. In this way, both will begin to have a single flavour and the vehicle somehow moves forward in life.

MEMORY

Memory can make you sad or enlightened. Memory of events, experience of the changing and the limited will lead you to bondage. Memory of your self will liberate you. The ever-changing, relativity however good or bad it may be, will bring you bondage. The unchanging one reminds you of your self.

Memory of past events, worries of the world will diminish the infinity of the Self. You should know where you are and what you are. If you are in ignorance, it is only because of your memory. If you are enlightened, that too is because of your memory. Very trivial things, incidents and sadness, forgetting all this is bliss. Forgetting the infinity is misery.

Qusetion: How to resolve lack and overcome painful memories?

Sri Sri: There are many ways to do this:

1. Understanding clearly that everything in the world is impermanent.

2. Understanding that events which happened in the past are no more living or real now and accepting those events.

3. Having dispassion and being centered.

4. Remembering your Self and service of the noble minded.

5. Increasing your *prana,* 'sohum' or 'so what".

6. Divine company and Divine presence.

7. Go to the moon.

Question: What is infinity?

Sri Sri: That which is in-finite is infinity. There is infinity in everything which is finite. Are you aware of this? In every atom, the distance between two particles is equal to the distance between two galaxies. This means that the infinity is hidden in the finite. *Brahma* is hidden in every galaxy. Infinity is hidden in every atom.

'*Smruthir Labdva*' is commonly said. This what Arjuna said to *Krishna* after listening to the Gita. This means that after listening to so much of the Gita from *Krishna*, at the end of 700 or so stanzas and after asking so many questions - wanted or unwanted – in the end Arjuna says: *"Smruthir labdva, karishye vachanam tava."* I have remembered now. I will do whatever you say. He did not say thank you to *Krishna*. He said that he remembered.

It means that everything is there in the memory. Memory gives enlightenment to your life. What do we say when we get enlightened? We say that we remembered. It means that we have remembered our true nature.

There was once this beggar who would go round begging from people. He belonged to the royal family and for some reason he had forgotten that he was the prince and lived by begging. A soldier of the King found him and reminded the prince of his former state. He told him, "You are a prince. The king is looking for you."

The moment the prince got back the memory of himself, that very moment his actions, mannerisms, way of walking, talking, thinking and behaviour under went rapid transformation. The same person who would go to people and ask for 5 or 10 rupees to drink tea became a commander in the next instant and had the bravery to question people.

Similarly, when you regain the memory of 'who am I?' all the meekness in you will disappear. You will walk with high spirits. 'Who am I?' I am God's son or daughter. So why should I experience lack of anything? The whole world is there for me. What can time do to me? This sort of genuine bravery should arise in you. 'I am really the child of immortality - *Amruthasya putra* - I have no end' is the brave thought which should arise in you.

When will the bravery come, in your next birth? You should get it the moment you are in the presence of the *Guru*. The thought that we have a *Guru* should bring braveness in you. How is it not possible to become brave? You have not seen or experienced God. But when you have someone to call your own, why the fear? When the King himself is your man, you can walk like the Prime Minister. Anyway all kings have a lot of headaches, but their secretaries, personal assistants and drivers, their heads will not stand still. They are always in high spirits. If God wants to worry let him do so. You be in peace.

We should walk with such courage and enthusiasm. When will this happen? This happens because of memory. You should feel that God belongs to you. You visit temples like you visit a bus terminal. It is all so impersonal. You never feel that God is yours. You think he resides somewhere in the temple. You should feel that 'God is mine and he resides in my mind'. The moment this feeling arises in you, you get all the bravery needed in your life. All the meekness will vanish. Whatever we desire and whatever we need will begin to happen. Whatever is right, necessary and good will happen.

So what happens because of memory? We can become ignorant or enlightened. You become the enlightened one by memory of your Self. We also become ignorant because of memory. If you keep thinking of all that is unwanted and heating up your head thinking: "He said this, he said that, how arrogant is he to talk to me in this way. They did this to me at the wedding…" Remembering such trivial things and living with them is ignorance.

Why do you feel sad? You desired something the day before yesterday. Your wish from four days ago was not fulfilled. The memory of your past desire is now causing you sadness. How is it possible to be sad when you do not remember? You may feel the pain, but you will not be sad. When does the mind feel sad? When there is memory. So, because of memory you can be enlightened and because of memory you become ignorant too.

SURRENDER AND ACCEPT

Whatever exists in this Universe, be it big or small, all objects have the Divine's voice in them. By understanding, by knowing that Divine's voice is pervading all over the Universe, by knowing that all the chocolates present inside the chocolate box are only chocolates, how does the wrapping paper of the chocolate appear to you? You will realise that the wrapping paper is only external. What is present inside the wrapping paper is all Divine. When such a realization dawns on you, then you will not get into differentiating things. You feel, "What is a wrapping paper after all? What difference does it make if this wrapping paper is nice, if that is blue wrapping paper and this is red wrapping paper?"

The Divine's voice is present inside every wrapping paper. Whatever type the wrapping paper may be, whatever shape and form it may have like the China dolls, what difference does it make? They do many varieties of biscuit dolls in China. Even though there are many varieties of animals, they are all biscuits.

Whatever exists in this Universe everything is the place of Divine's residence.

Eeshaavaasyam idam sarvam
Yat kincha jagatyaam jagat
Yena tyaktena bhunjeeta
Maa grudhaha kasyaswaiddhanam
(Eeshavasyopanishad. Mantra)

"Whatever is living in this Universe, *Shiva* resides in all these being. First surrender and then accept. Do not wish for other's wealth."

It means, even though the Divine resides in every object, by holding on to any object you will end up in delusion. You will be miserable. What should be done? You should surrender everything. You can only surrender whatever you consider as yours. Isn't it? What can you sacrifice? You can only sacrifice whatever you are holding on to. Whatever you are holding onto, you cannot even enjoy it. If you hold something in your hands and keep thinking "mine, mine" e.g. if you are holding a sweet tightly in your fists and saying "mine, mine", it is of no use. It is over the moment you eat it. If you neither eat it yourself nor give it to others, even though you are hungry, yet you do not want to let it go, it will not be of any use in your fists.

First surrender and then accept. If you sacrifice and then accept anything, it then becomes *prasaad,* the Divine's gift.

Whatever you accept as Divine's gift, you will not exercise your right on it. You will consider yourself as blessed whereas if you hold on to any object considering it as your right, "I have got it. I have done it. Mine"… If you live with this feeling, you cannot actually enjoy it. If you decide to enjoy it with this feeling, you will not derive any happiness from it. You will only be miserable.

If you keep thinking "my son, my son", you get misery from that very son. Even after having a son like *Shri Ramachandra,* when *Dasharatha* himself could not get happiness, can you get any other happiness? Did *Vasudeva* get any happiness even after getting a son like *Krishna?* So, instead of being miserable by thinking "my son, my son", think, "Let everything happen as per Divine's wish. Everything anyway belongs to the Divine." If you have this feeling, that will not bring you misery. Offer back all the objects whatever you have in this world to the Divine. Offer everything. This is sacrifice.

Even though God resides in everything, first surrender and then accept. Nothing here belongs to any body. Do not feel jealous, do not hate anybody. If at all people decide to sacrifice something, they do so after becoming miserable and beaten. You cannot consider that as a sacrifice by them. If you do not like ladies finger and you throw it out and say, "I have sacrificed", then that is not sacrifice. You do not even like it in the first place! If one is in too much love with anything, first surrender that and then accept it. Whatever you enjoy after offering, the happiness you get out of it is many times greater. If you keep exercising your authority by saying "mine, mine", you will get no happiness from it.

TENDENCIES OF THE MIND

See now what is happening in the mind? Are you aware what is happening in the mind right now?

There is an expectation - what next? What is going to be spoken? Now, whatever I say there are only two options, either you agree with me or disagree with me, isn't it? In either case it doesn't matter what it is, does it?

But are we aware of our agreement or disagreement? This matters too. See what I am saying? Now I have spoken a few sentences and even before I complete the sentences your mind is already in dialogue. I am speaking in the mind but you are also speaking in your own mind. Do you notice that? Your mind says, 'yes-yes, right, no-no, how can it be?'

Education is being aware of this phenomenon of the mind. What is happening in our mind right now? All other information we can acquire reading books? You can open a book on any subject - on birth or death or children - there are volumes and volumes of books. Libraries are filled with books.

In fact we know all about it, mostly everybody knows, but what we need to give attention to, is this awareness of our own mind. What does our mind do? It vacillates between past and the future. Every moment, it either goes to the past or to the future. It is angry about the past, about what has already happened. All our anger is about that which has already happened, finished or it is anxious about the future, which is not there right now. This is the oscillation of the mind.

And then the mind has another tendency i.e. clinging on to the negative. You say everything is fine, but... If you remember, you use it very often, 'Oh he is a nice guy or a nice lady, but...' We put a break there, but. If there are ten positive instances or events and one negative thing happens, we cling on to that one negative thing and leave all the ten positive. Have you observed this tendency of the mind? Ten years of friendship and a few days of arguments, that is it! The balance is stopped.

The only self-help we can do is to bring a change to these two tendencies of the mind. Be aware of this tendency in the mind and whenever you are trying to say, 'but' just be aware. 'Oh I am trying to say "but" now.' And that will make you very natural, simple, and open from inside. It is very precious in life.

The most precious thing in life is to maintain the innocence, which we have. We are born with some innocence in us, as we become more and more intelligent, we tend to lose the innocence and try to become a little more stiff. Drop the stiffness, then life will be much more rewarding, more enjoyable, more interesting. And that is worship.

Five factors bring about completion in life. Any one of the five factors can bring about completion in life. Can you guess what these five factors are?

Even if we think that whatever we require, we have it all with us, we still require these five factors to make our life complete, to fill our lives. Love is life's completion. That is the goal of life. How to reach the goal? How to attain it? What are the means to attain it? What are the things required in order to say that your life is complete? These are the five factors:

The first one is *shraddha* (faith). Life cannot progress if there is no faith. Isn't it? You have to believe in the people around you. You have to have faith in the laws of nature. You have no choice, but to have faith in the laws of nature. Otherwise, you will begin to have the desire to know what will happen when. Entire science is based on that one thing, the law of nature. Belief in people around you, belief in the world, belief in that something which cannot be seen behind all this is the belief in nature.

Now, you trust a person but you cannot see the mind of that person. Yet you believe in the mind of that person. Isn't it? Now, you are looking at nature, you believe on a very subtle level and that is known as God or *Parabrahma*. Whatever you call it, believe in it. All thoughts and everything else arise from it. When you are filled with complete belief, then you feel you are complete. If there is a lack of faith in your life, then such a life is incomplete. Such a life will be filled with worries, anxieties and sadness.

A very stressful mind can never be happy, cannot be in love and cannot achieve anything in the world. Isn't it? Therefore, faith completes your life. Believe that everything good will happen to you in future. Believe the divinity. Faith is one factor.

The second is *smriti* (memory). What you do, where were you born, remembering all these... Many of you will not even be aware that you are born. You just live. We celebrate our birthdays. "Oh! What gifts should I get today?" or "What gift should I give?" All your attention is merely on the gift rather than on your life. It probably happened in the past, if somebody remembered, "Oh! I was born this day" and sat and felt sad about it, in order to console them, people would probably give them some gift to make them forget about their birthday. People would probably sit and regret: "Oh! I have spent forty, fifty years of my life in a wasteful manner." When they would have been sadly remembering, "I could neither achieve anything in life nor could live it happily," people would probably give them gifts and distract them from their sorrow. The person who would receive the gift would then forget the sorrow and would become immersed in the gift.

Most people are living in this world without being aware of their source. "How was life formed? How did we come to this world?" No such thoughts arise in them. The knowledge of us arriving into this world, knowledge of birth and knowledge of death; no such knowledge exists in them. They live as though they are going to live here forever. Every body or even if few people realize that we are not going to live here forever is enough for them for them to lead happier lives. They will then neither land themselves in trouble nor trouble others. Don't you think so?

There is lack of awareness of one's origin i.e. not being aware that we will go away from this earth, living in the delusion that everything is forever, living without being aware of the present moment. "I am living. What is there in this body? Who am I really?" Are you all at least aware as to where you are, here in Wilson Garden, in the eighth cross? But are you aware that you are in Bangalore? Are you aware that you are in Karnataka? Are you aware that you are in India? Are you aware that you are in the Asian Continent? Are you aware that you are living on this earth? You have not even thought about it. Are you aware that you are living in the solar system? Are you aware that you are also a part of this milky way? Lack of awareness about existence.

We have no awareness of time. We have no awareness about what is there in our body, no awareness of space and time. This body is made up of many substances. Are you aware of this? Do you know this? Blood is circulating constantly in your body. Are you aware of your heart beat? Have you ever experienced your heart beat?

Even when you are anxious, you become so involved in the circumstances and never experience the sensations. Isn't it? We are not aware of what is happening to our body. Isn't it? We are not aware! This moment of ours, the past or the future will not exist in our memory. This is very obvious.

When you remember, you will become aware that you are living in this world as if you are waiting in the waiting area in the airport. You come carrying your suitcases. Before boarding the plane you wait in the waiting room for two, three or five hours. You have to shift from one train to the other. You have to go somewhere, say you have to go to Nasik. For that you need to go to Pune and change your train there. For that, you will not open all of your luggage in the railway station itself. Awareness of time, awareness of the place where we are living, when these come our life becomes complete, it becomes perfect.

The third is *veerya* (valour or bravery) and refers to one hundred percent bravery, the bravery to renounce. Do you understand what I am saying? Have you seen the people in the army? Or people who have dedicated their lives 100%? Have you seen terrorists? If you observe subtly you can see some attraction in it, some energy in it.

Many people are not aware what it is to be a terrorist. Terrorists put their 100%. They dedicate their own lives, but they are always nagged by some worry inside them. This is because of the ignorance in them. The path they have chosen is the wrong one. Stress and worries trouble them a lot. When there is no stress and worry and when there is a shine, it is known as valour.

What will be happening to powerful people like Veerapandi Kattabomman (a warrior king who has attained a legendary status in Tamil Nadu) or Kittur Chennamma (the queen of Kittor in Karnataka known for her valour), or some other powerful person? Come what may, they put their 100%. That is *veerya*. You can see that valour, that energy, that prowess in them. You can see that much of energy, fearlessness, complete centeredness and full flow of energy in an enlightened one, without any obstacles or fear.

The fourth one is *samadhi*. What is *samadhi*? When the mind is in equanimity, in a peaceful state, when it is unshakeable, that is *samadhi*. Even if the mind shakes for a little while, it comes back to its center almost immediately. This state of the mind is known as *samadhi*. The mind is neither clinging to the past nor it is worried about the future, the mind which does not fall into the shackles of anger, hatred and craving. No hatred of anything nor craving for anything. Do you understand this?

There are no cravings, feverishness or hatred in such a mind. "That is not right. I do not want that, I want only this. I cannot stand this." A mind which has none of these, such a state of mind is *samadhi*. There are no regrets, no anger and no fear. *Samadhi* does not mean sitting in one corner doing nothing.

There are many types of *samadhi*. 'S*amatvam yogam uchyate*' means equanimity in the mind, harmony in the mind. Such a mind which has harmony and balance is one factor which brings about completion in life.

Last one is *pragna* which means awareness, having a full mind. Whatever you do, doing it with a complete mind, even if you are scolding someone, scolding them with full awareness. Are you getting this? When we get angry, we lose our mind. Even when we are praising someone, we lose our mind. So, being aware all the time is *pragna*.

So *shradda* (faith), *smruti* (memory), *veerya* (valour), *samadhi* and *pragna* (awareness), these five factors complete life.

Now you can ask questions, this is the art of living and if you can follow this at least to some extent, if you can practise at least one or all of the factors, you can complete your life. Even if one happens it is enough, the others will follow automatically. When faith comes, when memory comes, when valour comes, *samadhi* happens. *Pragna* will come, everything will come.

Question: How to develop this thing called faith?
Sri Sri: Okay, now, how do you develop doubts? Keep a watch on your doubts and then faith grows on its own. Look at the nature of your doubts. You always doubt only what is good. If somebody comes and tells you that such and such a person is bad, you never even doubt the badness of that person. Isn't it? You never doubt negativity.

If anybody comes and says, "I am really angry with you," then you will never doubt it, whereas if somebody comes and says, "I love you very much," then you doubt that. You say "Really?" You say,

"What do you want from me?" You doubt your positivity and you doubt your capabilities e.g. you are very sure that you cannot climb ten floors, "Oh! I cannot do that. I tried to climb two floors and my legs are aching. How can I climb ten floors now? Not possible." You doubt your capabilities and place faith in your in-capabilities.

Doubt people's negativity. Do you understand this? If anybody is saying something out of stress and anxiety, you accept it as it is. You just assume that they are bad people. When you peep into every bad person, you can find a good person sitting inside. People, under the influence of stress behave in a negative manner, due to their ignorance. When you begin to doubt negativity, then you will believe the positive. If you assume that everybody in the world are useless and begin to look for who is trust worthy and where they are, then you will never find such a person. Usually we live life with this attitude. If you think, "Everybody is good but if they are bad it is because of some reason, let us see what the reason is," then it is such a beautiful thing.

By understanding doubt, faith happens. Another way is, when your *prana* levels are very low, your consciousness becomes doubtful. When you do good *pranayams* and *kriya* there will be no doubts in your mind. Have you observed this? Then your mind is clear and straight. This is because of the energy in you increasing without any blocks. When there is a block in the flow of *prana*, you begin to doubt yourself. Doubt in yourself, doubt in people around you and doubt in the existence of the Divine arise in you. Increase the *prana* and awareness. Both of these will resolve the doubts.

Question: Is there any easy method to obtain all these five factors?
Sri Sri: Do a little *pranayama*, a little meditation. You have to do some practical things too. Okay, now we gave you a discourse. But, you need to do something for your body and mind too. See, there are seven levels to our existence. They are: body, breath, mind, intellect, memory, ego and the Self. A little knowledge and little help form the Self. All our other activities take place only with the help of the Self. That is why, if we increase the *prana* and energy in us, we can rise to great levels. We can achieve a lot in life.

ARE YOU MERE HUSK OR THE GRAIN?

During the time of reaping the harvest, the farmer holds a broad sieve and puts all the grain into it and stands on an elevated platform and shakes the sieve. What happens when that is done? Have you seen this scene? What happens? If it is mere husk, it just flies away in the air and is lost. If grain is present, then it falls to the ground and stays.

So too in our life, we must have faith. What? Faith. Faith is something which we have inside us. When many situations surface in life, are you able to face all of them with peace, with a stable mind and faith? If you do not have faith, if you go into fear, then you will fly away into the air, like the husk. You will be nowhere. You will not have anything to hold onto. Such people will have no value at all.

But if you have faith, you will be able to find ground. When you have faith that every thing be alright, when you are in peace, then everything will settle down.

God expects only one thing from you, "Your unshakeable faith." If your faith shakes very quickly, if it keeps shaking too often, or if you realize that you do not have any faith at all when difficulty strikes, then it is akin to being like the husk. The rest is whether "you are mere husk or the grain"?

How many events take place in life! Many situations arise. Are you able to maintain your equanimity in those conditions? Your work is to maintain your equanimity in this world. Not everything in the world is sweet; somethings are sweet and somethings are bitter. If you are grounded with faith like the husk with grain, then you will progress. The grounded grains are gathered in a sack and re-planted else where or used in some manner.

Take this decision, "Whatever happens I will be there. I will be grounded. God's protection is there on me. Whatever happens, I will never go down. I always have God's hand with me." This much is enough to pull you up. Keep your mind in peace in all situations. It is enough if that much is done by you. We will take care of everything else.

Maintain your equanimity. You have to do only this. It is not right if we have to do everything and you do nothing. Not possible. You have to take at least one step forward. Be in peace and equanimity. "Oh, nothing happened. None of my work happened" – if you are able to laugh in such a situation, then understand that you have protection with you. The world is filled with love. Everybody has love inside them. You have to see that in your mind.

Have you ever seen with this view? Whenever you are in a crowd, have you ever watched the crowd and thought in your mind that 'all is love'? Once think in this manner and look, either today or tomorrow or some day. Even now there is a crowd. Just once look at everybody in this crowd and feel the love present in everybody.

The whole world is a celebration. Fair happens here constantly, celebration happens here everyday. Parrot, cuckoo and other birds sing and play *naadaswaram* (a South Indian traditional instrument like a trumpet). All the birds play *naadaswaram*. Procession is moving constantly. We are the idols who are moving in the procession. So for once think that everybody is love.

You should be happy in life. All other businesses involve ups and downs; all that is natural. If there is a body, then it will get a cold, cough, fever or something else and it will go away. But take care to see that happiness is always established in you. That is known as *purashaartha*. Our love, faith and belief should be deep-rooted; then everything else moves on its own.

FEAR OF FUTURE

Two villagers were sitting in a place. They were close friends. One said, "What are you thinking?" The other said, "I am planning to buy five acres of land, a garden." The other friend said, "Don't buy the garden." The first one asked, "Why?," the second said, "I am planning to buy a buffalo. Then my buffalo will enter your garden and we will fight, have misunderstandings and we will lose our friendship. I do not want to lose our friendship."

The first one said, "Okay then. You cancel your plan of buying a buffalo. I am going to buy my garden." The second one said, "No, no, no. I have already paid the deposit for my buffalo." The first one said, "How will your buffalo enter my garden? I will fence it thoroughly."

The second one said, "No, you see it can just enter. Buffalo is a buffalo. Who can stop it? It can do anything."

So a fight started, it went to such an extent… they fought each other, broke each other's limbs and went to the *Panchayat (*the village administrative body) and told them what happened. Neither had one brought a buffalo nor had the other bought any land. Nothing had happened. Just the mind's race and both of them broke their limbs over it!

Our fears are like that. The future has not yet come. We just sit there and think, "Oh! What will happen?" Finally you will die! This is what is going to happen! So much anxiety about the future! In this run the mind gets into such a mess. It is unable to see the presence that is all around you.

The mind totally forgets the Divine. "Me, mine, what about tomorrow, the day after and the day after that, next year, ten years later?" People plan in this way even up to the next birth! When people are newly married they say, "We are husband and wife for many lifetimes to come! This one birth is not enough. We will be man and wife for the next seven births!"

In reality, they will be fed up of each other in this birth itself. But they talk of the next seven births! After few days they will know. But the next seven births is what is told initially.

We should experience the Divine's presence, the Divine's light around us. You should have a desire in your mind to experience this. Have we ever desired for the Divine light? Has such a desire ever risen in you that you want the highest peace? Has it arisen from deep inside you? The Divine light, whatever that is, you do not know what it is. It is something by which the whole world is running. Have you ever really wanted it? When you sing or pray there should be total involvement. You don't involve yourself totally. Mind is pre-occupied elsewhere and something is happening. Then that is no prayer at all. There should be total involvement. When there is pain there is more involvement.

Somebody once told *Gurudev,* "You are a great renunciate. You have renounced everything. You are the greatest renunciate." *Gurudev* said, "No, no. I have renounced the greatest! You are the greatest renouncer. I bow down to your feet. You are sitting here after having lost the greatest of all. You have lost that from which everything else is created. Not just those which belong to you now but even those which are going to come in the future. They also arise from it. You do not ever thirst for it! You are sitting here, open-mouthed, for all the small little, insignificant things."

MIND AND TIME

Time and mind are connected and synonymous. *'Desha, Kala, Manah'* are three *tattvas* (principles). *'Desha'* is space, *'kala'* is time and, *'manah'* is mind. All these principles are connected. *Desha* and *kala* are connected; space and time are connected. For example, one day on the planet Earth is many days on the moon. So, if you are on Jupiter, one human year is only one month. On Jupiter if you experience one year, it is 12 years of Earthly time. Jupiter takes 12 years to go around the Sun. Similarly, if you are on the planet Saturn, 30 years is equivalent to one year.

Similarly, *'pitras'* are the people who have died; one human year is one day for them, so our six months are only one night and six months are one day. There are different times and different spaces in different dimensions. So, the time and space are connected. It's called the time-space curve. The same is with the third dimension that is mind. The mindless, transcendental consciousness is called '*Mahakala*', the *Shiva*, the fourth state of consciousness. *Mahakala*, means great time, and the no-mind; the no mind is great time.

Morning 4.30 to 6.30, just before sunrise, before dawn, is called the most creative time. '*Brahma muhurta*' and then every two hours is called a '*lagna*'; which means, one unit of time. This unit of time corresponds to the state of mind and this is connected with the moon's and the sun's position. There are ten different aspects which influence the mind. So, not only the time or hour of the day affects the mind but also the quality of the days affects the mind. Within every two and a half days, the mood of the mind changes, so if you are upset, it can continue for two and a half days at maximum; it may not stretch even to two and a half days. It rises to a peak and drops. But after two and a half days, you cannot have the same emotion with the same intensity. It is impossible, it changes, it switches. It is a great, great science - how mind, mood and time are connected.

'*Jyotish shastra*' (astrology) has deep insight into this. You know usually all these weekly column astrologers say, "Oh, good for relationships, making money", this and that. (Laughter) They generalise those things, "If you are born on this time then this is good for you and you should do this." Of course, it's too generic and it's just a money-making thing that they do. But it all is not just hoax; there is an iota of truth in it. The underlying base has some truth. The principle that the mind and time are connected is correct.

Mind means moods, thoughts, opinions, ideas, all these things that we collect. No mind is 'meditation'. Dawn and dusk are considered to be very good for mediation. Whenever you meditate you let go off the influence of the mind and go into the Self. So, whenever bad time is there you meditate. The Self is '*Shiva tattva*'; *Shiva tattva* means - always benevolent, caring, loving and uplifting. That consciousness deep within you which is caring, loving, uplifting and benevolent will nullify the negative influences of the mind and the time.

In India it is a very common belief, whenever there is bad time just say, '*Om Namah Shivaya*', and it's gone. '*Manah*', when read from the other side, becomes '*Namah*'. *Manah* is when consciousness goes outside in the world, and *Namah* is when the consciousness turns inwards towards the *Shivaya*, the *Shiva tattva* (*Shiva* principle), the fourth state of consciousness, the subtlest aspect of the existence. So, when the mind goes towards the basic substratum of creation, then it can have more uplifting experiences.

YOU HANDLE YOUR MIND

Lord *Krishna* says in *Gita*, "When a *yogi* sleeps, everybody is awake; when everyone is sleeping, a *yogi* is awake." What does it mean? It simply means, when everyone is excited and worried, the *yogi* sleeps comfortably. The *yogi* knows that everything will happen for the best and all happenings will be for the general good. A *yogi* has this confidence. "When everyone else is sleeping, then *yogi* is awake", means - the *yogi* is aware about the truth of life.

Nobody wonders, "What is going to be my end? Where will I go? What is life? Who am I?" If these questions don't arise in people's mind, then they are asleep. People are lost in watching movies and playing video games. People start playing video games even at very old age. Man isn't seeing that death is approaching. He does not think, "How I have filled my mind with so many cravings and aversions? I have done nothing to wash and cleanse my mind." If you don't clean impressions on the mind, then you have to carry the same mind and impressions with you after death.

So, when you die, your mind should be happy and joyful. One, who is sleeping, is carrying all the garbage in his mind. The *yogi* is alert and awake. He does not take any garbage from anybody in his mind; "Why this man said this to me or that lady said that to me?"

Your mind is completely destroyed thinking about others' imperfections. Leave others' imperfections to them only, let them handle. You handle your mind; you handle your imperfections and that is good enough. Do you have the patience to accept others' mistakes? You have to accept others' mistakes. If you are so compassionate, correct them as much as you can, then it doesn't get into your head, your mind. Otherwise leave it to the nature, it will find its own way.

When do you get angry or upset - when you see someone else's action as imperfect. Can you correct somebody's action like this? His action is imperfect but now thinking about it, your mind becomes imperfect. You save your mind at least. Others have gone on the wrong path, why should you let your mind also dwell on the wrong? Right? That is why He (*Krishna*) says, "The *yogi* is awake when others are sleeping." When you are sleeping, you let others' garbage enter into your mind. But *yogis* don't let this happen, they keep their mind fresh.

As your mind blossoms, new aspects of knowledge will blossom in you. Knowledge is structured in the consciousness.

Where does the mind go? It goes towards beauty, light, strength... Lord *Krishna* says, "Wherever your mind goes, see Me in that." If something is beautiful, it is because it has life in it. It is the same consciousness. So, the mind goes back to the source. Lord *Krishna* says, "The light in the sun is Me; I am the liquid in the water; I am the smell in the Earth; I am the fire in the fire."

We are made up of the same substance as the Sun. If there is no sun then there is no Earth and if there is no Earth then there will be no you too. If you talk to a quantum physicist, he will say the same thing: "Everything is made up of one wave function."

The same thing Lord *Krishna* said, "I am the life in everybody." Turn your mind inwards and look at the life force that you are. "In life, it is Me." Life is God. God is not something outside life. Life is Divine.

Life in this body is Divine. What is the mind craving for? For this pleasure or that pleasure. Right now, attend to life. Not that only my life is God, life everywhere is the same *Atma*.

REST YOUR MIND IN THE DIVINE

You can't say whether the body leads the mind or the mind leads the body. What you can say is: the body, breath and mind getting into a rhythm is *'Sudarshan kriya'*. Finding that inner harmony and depth, and manifesting on the physical level of the body and breath is 'meditation'. Through *mantra*, you go to the deepest level of your consciousness and bring it to expression in your day-to-day activity. This is meditation.

When you are content and not bombarded with your own needs, you gain the ability to bless. We need to learn the skill of being content. This can only happen through meditation. We have a beautiful tradition where we seek blessings from our elders on all festivals or occasions. This is very scientific. Ideally, elders are expected to be content, and hence they have the ability to bless. But today this is missing. Contentment does not mean being lethargic and not working, and also one need not wait till getting old to feel contented. A wave of contentment should spring in the mind. Keep doing your work but have a sense of satisfaction in the mind. Some point of time in life, one should reach the stage of feeling, "I am contented." Without contentment, power to bless cannot get awaken in you. Many people who have done the Blessing course had this experience that if they wished good for others, it got accomplished. Celebrate and enjoy your life, do *Sadhana*, *Seva* and *Satsang*. Be happy and make others happy.

Our scriptures provide three main philosophies:
1. *Nyaaya* (Logic)
2. *Vaisheshika*
3. *Sankhya*
After that we have *Yoga*.

Nyaaya: Whatever we learn, we understand and analyse how correct it is. '*Nyaaya*' is analysing the difference between what we hear and what we infer. This is a way of finding out the truth.

Vaisheshika: In the *'Vaisheshika'* method, the object and its characteristics are analysed. If sugar is not sweet, will you still call it sugar? Objects have characteristics. In this way, place and time are also considered as objects because of their characteristics. Time affects the mind and intellect. Our mind feels and perceives differently in the morning than in the evening. The placement of the planets also affects the mind. Sometimes faith arises in the mind, sometimes hatred envelopes the mind. It is natural for different waves of emotions to rise in the mind. I am separate from all this, I am *Atma*. Contemplating on this is a sign of intelligence.

Once you have understood that the objects are changing, rest your mind on that which never changes. This is *Sankhya Yoga*.

What is *Bhakti*? *Bhakti* is resting your mind and intellect in the Divine energy. That's all that you need to do. Whenever your faith shakes cure it by taking blessings from the elders or do *yoga*.

To calm the mind be friendly and compassionate, and finally ignore if needed. Ignore the imperfections and keep your mind calm. Hating somebody is like drinking poison and do not ever hate wise people. *Patanjali* says, "Awake the opposite emotion." This is *sadhana*. If anger arises, awake compassion, a new chemical process will initiate.

'Vitarka badhane, pratipaksha bhavanam.'

That is why we remember the *Guru* - the chemical process changes immediately, and enthusiasm, joy and non-attachment arise naturally.

SAVE THE MIND AT ANY COST

The whole world is made up of five elements. Honouring the Earth element means - we don't pollute the Earth with plastics, poisonous fertilizers and chemicals. It means that we are environment conscious.

Honouring water does not mean putting flowers into the water. There is a shortage of clean drinking water. First, we pollute the water and then the water pollutes the Earth. In the last century, people did not know anything about soaps. In this country (India), people were using only charcoal ashes, soap nut powder to clean vessels. They were using turmeric and other herbal elements, which are bio-degradable.

There is a great tradition of honouring rivers. The river does not want you to offer flowers or fruits. This is not the way of doing *pooja* (worship). By putting sewage or garbage into rivers, how can you say that you are doing *pooja*? *Pooja* means honouring and you can only do full honour once you stop dumping sewage, garbage, plastic into the rivers.

Nowhere in the scriptures it is mentioned that you have to put the flowers or fruits into the river. Of course, one way of honouring is with flowers and they are bio-degradable. However you should stop dumping garbage.

A few years ago you could directly drink water from a river. Today, no river is fit for drinking even from a hundred kilometers away from its source. Earlier, even a thousand kilometres away from its source, the river water was fit for drinking. We are pouring so much of industrial waste into the rivers. This is not honouring the *jal tattva* (water element). The five elements are part of this creation. You have to honour and sustain this beautiful creation.

Then there is the 'air element'. We need to have clean source of energy. We have provided smokeless stoves in the villages of Maharashtra, which have been very successful.

Then there is the 'space element'. It is very abstract. You cannot catch space. When you save your mind from negativity, you are filling the space with joy. Then the air around you becomes like that. You can create a space of mistrust, anger, greed, jealousy and selfishness or you could create a space of fun, joy, confidence and coherence. You could create an accommodating space around you and if you always speak negative about mistakes, then is Earth you can really survive. Everybody is imperfect. When we try to see perfection in others, then we forget to see our own imperfections. Protect the space; save the mind at any cost.

IT'S ALL ME

In the *Gita* it is said that even the most brilliant people are confused about what to do and what not to, and how to handle the mind. It is a big job. Protecting the mind is a great task unless you do it with knowledge. Till this moment, see all that has happened so far. It's all gone; finished.

Wake up. When you are full of energy, *prana*, you see it's all gone. Now all that happened seems okay. Think about what to do now. Sometimes what you do will be successful and sometimes it will not be. A farmer knows that every seed he is sowing will not sprout. He throws the seeds in the field and does not worry which will sprout and which will not.

From now, it's a new chapter. Every day is a new chapter. Bring up this awareness again and again. The whole world is filled with my *atma* (soul) – it's all Me. It's one *chetna* (Consciousness). This one consciousness works through one person in one way, through another person in some other way. It is an ocean with many waves.

If this vision comes to you even just for five seconds then there will be a major transformation in your body and mind. Then a realization will spring in you '*Aho*!'

All worries are washed off. Just for a second, recognize that it's only Me in my enemy. I myself have started this game. Understand this but don't turn it into a mood making. Have this understanding only in the *nivriti* but not in the *pravritti* mode. If we bring *advaita* (non-duality) in *vyavahar* (behaviour), we only create more *bhrama* (delusion). In *pravritti*, see duality.

Taking up of the human form is impossible without *pravritti*. How much *pravritti* and *nivriti* one should have is a very sensitive matter. When there is more *pravritti*, then one becomes too negative and one is asked to be in *nivriti*.

In India, *dand* (punishment) is called *shiksha* (education). The word *saja* (punishment) comes from *shiksha* (education). Earlier one was not punished out of anger but out of compassion. When there would be too much *pravritti* in someone they would put him in a room (jail) and provide food, sleep and rest. Like the doctor admits people in hospital when the body becomes sick, when our *kritya* (action) is sick then the *karta* (doer) is sent to jail.

When you have both, *pravritti* and *nivriti* then you are successful.

YOU CAN'T MAKE ANYBODY HAPPY

I have seen that *swamis*, *sadhus* and people in ancient times did not like listening to any conflict. If someone complained to them they would just plug their ears and say, "You deal with it." See, if you are part of the solution, your energy is high. But if you are talking only about problems, your energy comes down.

In this world there is always a play of positive and negative. Some problems come, some challenges come and solutions also follow them. The ancient people would simply focus on keeping their energy high. If your energy is high and people come to you, their problems will get solved.

What happens when people talk to you about their problems? You get steeped in their problems. You get carried away with the problems. So just try this: let everybody come and complain 100 things to you, you simply keep your energy high, your sight inwards, your mind inwards as though nothing has happened. You will realise that there is freedom within you.

Try this - at home, your mother-in-law will complain, your husband will complain, anybody can complain about anything, let the world go topsy-turvy, but hold onto the idea - I am going to keep my energy high. You just take one such step and then see. Problems and challenges come so that you can turn your mind inwards. Instead of turning the mind inwards when problems come, what we do? We chase the problem and get completely drawn in that direction, and then our energy goes down and we collapse.

Many a times, in the name of compassion and sympathy you get drowned. Your compassion does not really help at all in solving the problem. It may sound very shocking but in compassion the problem multiplies, and doesn't get solved.

Problems come so that a person can turn inwards and look inside, get into a state of dispassion and calmness. Instead you give reasons and try to pacify the person. Pacifying a person in a problem is the worst thing. You should not pacify them. Let everybody carry their own cross. Bear their *karma*. If you are miserable or happy it is your *karma*. So you change your *karma*. This attitude makes a person more independent.

You show compassion and then they seek more attention. You feel more compassion and give them more attention and then neither compassion nor attention is possible. It breeds tension in you, "That poor person is so upset and I have to make him happy." To make someone happy is a big burden. Don't try to do that at all. This is a new policy - don't try to make anybody happy, you can't.

There is a Sanskrit proverb that says *'Kashtasya sukasya nakopi data'* - nobody gives happiness or misery. It is created by one's own self, one's own mind. When someone says 'problem', just turn and run in the other direction. Say, "You deal with your own problem." Then independence comes, Self-dependence comes in people and that is how you make yourself self-sufficient.

I am talking about this to *sadhaks*, to all of you, who are already on the path. "*Guruji* said let them deal with it, I am out of it." If you have space in your car, you should help them. Compassion is needed there, but not in relationships. When you are relating with people, random acts of compassion are essential. Be compassionate with someone whom you do not know. Be passionate about dispassion. Just see your own mind gets bogged down by others' feelings, tensions, miseries and unhappiness. What can you do? Where have you gone? What has happened to you? You are completely shattered. Cut all these cobwebs around you, all these strings around you, keep only one string - to the Divine.

Even there, don't say, "*Guruji* didn't look at me, maybe God is angry with me," No. Everything is *prasad*; if I am kicked out, it is also *prasad*; if I am scolded, it is *prasad*. Everything is *prasad*, this attitude is the best attitude. So, no attention - no tension. Good.

PERFECTION IN MIND

Our voice should be strong. The voice of truth and religion is weak. When the voice of violence is strong, it creates trouble. When the voice of love is strong and the voice of violence becomes weak, then that age is *Satyayuga* (the age of truth). The voice of Lord *Rama* should be stronger than *Ravana's*. Only then he can win. The same is with Lord *Krishna*.

When life feels like a struggle then we must focus on knowledge. Even *Arjuna* was told to be in the knowledge and meditation first and then fight. Always be in knowledge and then work.

To get knowledge we need not to go to the Himalayas. Knowledge can come even in the everyday life activities. Wanting perfection in work sometimes creates anger. If somebody does something wrong, it can create anger.

There are three types of perfection:
1. Perfection in mind keeps our mind in peace.
2. Perfection in speech is to speak only when needed. Don't get into fights.
3. Perfection in action - perfection in action is not 100 percent possible.

However, perfection in the mind and speech can be obtained by *sadhana* (spiritual practices), *seva* (service) and *satsang* (music and meditation). Once our mind and speech are perfect, work will also become perfect automatically.

It is the culture of India to accommodate everyone. Nobody is other disparate. Everybody is our own. For instance, the *Guru Granth* Sahib expresses *Brahmagyan* in simple language. This is a special aspect of India. We should not confine this knowledge only to us. We should share it with all so that everybody gets the benefit.

Often people ask, "Why do we pray to so many Gods and Goddesses?" The *Paramatma* (the Divine) is one, yet called by different names. Likewise with the same flour we can make either noodles or samosa (an Indian snack) or anything else. It is still the same flour. In the same way, it is the same *Paramatma* that we evoke through different names, forms and colours.

The meaning of *'aarti'* is complete happiness. Only when our life revolves around God, we get complete happiness. We should understand the right meaning of all the rituals. Then we will be happy and make others also happy. We have to get rid of unhappiness. We should do *pranayama*; focus on our breath everyday for 10 minutes or so. This is called *'pranayama'* and *'kriya'*. Through this, one can experience bliss and to be in bliss is total rest. The kriya helps to maintain health as well as purifies the mind, intellect and emotions. It helps us to come out of our guilt and be in the present moment. Do you use a cell phone? If you keep on pressing numbers but there is no SIM card inside, will it work? Now if you have a SIM card and no range, will it work? If the range and SIM card are there, but phone is not charged, will it work?

Sadhana is the SIM card, range is faith. If you prayed and claim that God didn't hear, means you don't have a SIM card. No prayer will work. *Satsang* is the charge. Temples and *Gurudwaras* are the places to get charged up. If we fight in a Temple or *Gurudwara*, then also the pure energy will be lost. God will not be there.

God comes where all are happy. When the mind is happy, our work gets done and we are able to bless others or heal them. All powers are hidden within the Self; *atma gyan* (Self knowledge) can bring them out. If you bless people, everything will manifest. If you have a cell phone but don't dial the number, will you get connected? You have to connect to yourself, your *prakriti* (nature), *atma* and *paramatma*, and then everything will manifest. That is why we have made a lot of blessers. Blessers are already happy. They can bless people and heal them.

A village has been transformed from a very badly reputed place in Maharashtra, India to a model village. People were afraid to go there. Now everyday 700 families come for *satsang*. We have found that there is no need of locks in that village anymore. There is a store with no store-keeper. People go there to buy food, and they put the total billed amount of the commodities taken in the box. This has become a model village with clean water and every house is coloured in pink. People do the cleaning on their own. They have switched to organic farming. There is no chemical farming. Everybody is employed. For the past three years this village has been working like this and 180 more villages are on the same track. Nobody drinks alcohol or smokes.

We can make this dream a reality. We can make it happen. We have got everything; keep your mind free, clean and pure. My only condition is that you leave all your tensions, stresses, worries and pains, and go home with a smile. Life is to be lived with happiness. We should neither remain sad nor make others sad. Leave all your unhappiness here. I am here only to remind you that God is there and He is your very own.

Thirty minutes of meditation will make you look brighter. We should all meditate for thirty minutes every day. We should all go to temples and sit there with our eyes closed for a few minutes.

CONTRADICTIONS IN THE MIND

Long, protracted, deep uninterupted meditation is the key to live fully the nature of the Self. Deep meditation, you have noticed every time you sit for meditation, you go a little deep, and then something happens, the thoughts come, all the deep impressions come out and then the mind comes out again, the depth is lost. Over and over, again and again as you practice meditation, you find your whole nature has changed. Those of you who began on meditation, would notice, as you move forward, the process of meditation is taking its own course. It's own twists and turns, it'a own depth. It is a process. So, don't stop till you reach the goal. What is the goal? The goal is when you feel no difference between in and out. And when you find yourself as a bubbling fountain of joy, of love, of awareness. Deep and protracted meditation, then you find that there are no two, the non-dual you, you are in and you are out. You are not the body, you are not the thoughts, you are not the feelings, you are the peace, you are the joy.

In deep sleep the *vrittis* get absorbed in the root ignorance. There is no super-intuitional knowledge as the mind is present there. In *nirvikalpa samadhi* one gets knowledge of the non dual *Brahman*. The *Brahmakara vritti* gets dissolved in *Brahman*. Of course sleep is something which is very similar to meditation. In sleep also there are no two, you are in the non-dual state but there is no awareness. Just like in sleep, where you are not aware of anything, but when you come out of the sleep you say, it was wonderful, so blissful. Every time you take a dip in the sleeping state of consciousness, you come out fresh, peaceful, relaxed and happy. Sleep provides you with some of the things that *samadhi* would provide. But *samadhi* or meditation provides something much more, that sleep can not give.

A few minutes of *nirvikalpa samadhi* means that state of deep meditation, the culmination of meditation where there are no thoughts, there is no duality, gives you the nectar of existence. That state brings you the nectar of life, that bliss. The moment you hear 'bliss' and 'nectar' the mind goes, "Oh I want it, I want it, how can I have it?" The craving in the mind begins for that. Arrest that tendency of the mind.

Withdraw the mind again and again from all the sense objects. Make it one-pointed. Fix it again and again on the self. Become fearless, attaining the Divine consciousness. Be firm in the world of Divine life. Self is not an object of the senses, Self is the experiencer of the objects of the senses. So again and again, withdraw your mind that runs around. If your mind is running all over the place, it's because of the objects of the senses. You want to look at something, you want to hear about something. All that you want to hear is something nice about yourself, from so many corners, from so many people's mouths. Or you want to look at something nice, that you can possess, you can touch, hold onto, you can grab and keep it to yourself. These are the two main things: hearing and seeing. The other three senses just tag on, smell, taste and touch.

When you feel that right now, I am not interested in looking at anything, I am not interested in seeing anything, I am not interested in hearing anything, not interested in smelling, tasting or touching anything; I am returning to my source. So bring the mind which is all over the place, back to its source. Withdrawing, with certain skill. You have to achieve this practice, just like you learn to speak a language, just like you learn to use the computer, just like you learn to drive a car or plane, you have to learn to retrieve back to the source. This is *sadhana*, this is a practice, this is something that comes to you not just by nature, but by your efforts. Again and again, bring your mind back to its source.

Drop the fear. Fear is always about the unknown and the most unknown for you is yourself. So, there is a fear there, "Oh, what will happen to me?" The element of divinity will take out the fear. One can meditate without a feeling of divinity, it is possible. They can mechanically sit, just like a technique do and the mind will become calm, but then the fear will take over. One can not go so deep, if he goes a little deep, then fear comes up. When you sit with feeling of the Divine, then the meditation goes so deep.

Sacredness, is the secret of the universe. In the womb of sacredness, creation happens. Consciousness is sacred. Sacredness is acknowledging the supermacy of nature. Sacredness is feeling the gratitude for this existence. Sacredness is acknowledging the infinite possibility of the intelligence. Sacredness is feeling the gratitude for this existence and honouring this existence. Without the sense of honour or respect, you can not dive into the depths of this existence.

Be firm in your vow. You know, when you see people going on the motor rally or a running race, you will find the crowd in between waiting at all the different stages, simply waving and encouraging them, "Keep it up, keep it up." This shouting and encouragement all along the way gives such a spirit and enthusiasm for them to compete. Mind needs such an encouragement. Be steadfast, go ahead, its fine, you are okay. They need assurance again and again. Mind needs assurance to win or even to lose and this is an act where mind is losing itself. Even here it needs an encouragement. 'Destroying this mind' - it's completely opposite, it means be firm. How can you be firm, you are saying destroy the mind at the first place. In this irony there is truth. In this contradiction there is the manifestation of reality. This contradiction reminds the nature of mind. When you want to annihilate the mind, the mind will say 'no'. So be firm, be committed, then the mind will disappear.

Just as the mist disappears by the rays of the Sun, so also ignorance vanishes by the rays of wisdom, the rays of knowledge. When a bolt of energy is released from deep within you, all the chattering, all the thoughts, all those things simply vanish, 'the mind is gone'. You are simply a lump of bubbling energy. And this is exactly what happens when the first rays of sun comes, then the mist disappears; the ignorance vanishes.

Love for sensual objects is bondage. Distaste for objects of sense is release. Destroy the craving seed and attain the non-dual, blissful *Brahamanic* seed. Craving for sense object is the bondage. Their existence seems to have given you some pleasure, so it binds you now, you crave for it, and it gives you more and more pain. This is the nature of sense objects. They promise pleasure to begin with and they also gives you a little taste but then leaves you with pain and suffering. Now you are hooked, you can neither leave it nor have it. Even having is painful and leaving is painful. Doing anything is painful. This is the nature of sense objects; this is the nature of bondage. 'What is bondage?' -attachment and craving for the objects of senses. Whole life is a lesson. What is freedom? '*Virakti*' - lack of craving, detachment from the objects of senses.

A child craves for toffee or candy or ice cream and those things are child's life. If the candy is not there, it will yell and scream and go over the floor, bang the head on the door, it will bang it's fists on the floor, all sorts of things to get that piece of candy. But as an adult you don't bother, you don't worry even if you miss or skip a meal, it doesn't bother you at all, you don't sit and cry. You may think "Okay, well may be good for me to lose some weight." But a child can not do this, a child will cry and make a big thing out of it, even if it misses a meal. This is '*virakti*', what is *virakti*? - be unmindful of any pleasure. So what, if it's there or not, it does not matter, fine. Freedom from the pleasure is the real freedom. Pain does not bind you, it is the pleasure that binds you, and the bondage is painful. If you are bound, you are not bound by misery, you are bound by your cravings and pleasures. Liberation is freeing from your own pleasures, the grip of your pleasures.

You need not drop your hatred, if you can just drop your cravings. Burn the seed of craving that is in you, and then the non-dual *Brahman* is already available inside you. There is a throne, why don't you sit on that throne? It is for you. You are walking around in torn clothes, in shabby state, begging for things that any way belong to you. 'Stop being a beggar'. Craving is nothing but being like a beggar. Craving for pleasure is like being a beggar, who is begging and nobody is giving him anything. Wake up! You are the King. What pleasure do you want? That will beckon to you, fall at your feet. Don't be a slave of pleasure. Kick those begging bowls, and you will find your meal will come decorated in a silver plate to you. You are holding onto a begging bowl and nobody even drops a penny in it. As long as your hands are holding the begging bowl, you will not realise the silver plate that is coming in front of you. You might have noticed when people ask you, you don't feel like giving them, and when people say, "No I don't want, you feel like giving them." This is a general psychology, the homeless people who ask for food, nobody feels like feeding. People enjoy feeding people who are so well fed that they can't take a morsel more. Parties are given to those who have full stomachs. Gifts are given to those who do not want. The moment someone asks something from you, that asking makes you withdraw. This is true all over the world, irrespective of culture, nationality or race. Nature follows the same laws. The more you beg, the more you crave for something, the farther it goes away from you. The moment you drop it and just repose in your self you will find all those things comes to you, manifolds, multiplied. There is a word of Jesus, he says, "Those who have will be given more, and those who do not have whatever little they have will also be taken away from them." This is a law of nature. Don't run behind those little objects of senses. Take the seat on your heart and the rest shall come to you. Seek the kingdom first and all else shall be added to you.

With the growth of *Sankalpa* or thought, this world arises. If the *sankalpa* is destroyed then this universe will disappear. Extinction of the *sankalpas* alone is *moksha* or liberation. Our lives are all just intentions. Every step is intention, every move is out of intention. You intend to drink water, so you go to the kitchen; you intend to drive, so you get into the car. Life is ruled by intentions and if this mind is filled with millions of intentions, that much bigger mess the mind is, its because intensions contradict each other. Too many thoughts in your mind, all in so many directions, cancel out each other and create a big mess. You have a thought, "Okay, I will go to the car," then you get another thought, "No, I will not go to the car." You are in a conflict. You take two steps forward and then two steps back, and you reach nowhere. Most people are in a mess because of their own mind, their thoughts are not in order. They are all jumbled up, confused because in their minds they think, "What will give me greater joy, greater pleasure?" Come on, wake up! Nothing will give you greater joy or pleasure, all this will give you greater pain, one after another.

Where is the choice? The choice is only between bad and the worst. If you realise this you will drop both the conflicting thoughts and relax. The awareness becomes 'choiceless'. Choicelessness is the confusion free state of mind. Choiceless awareness is the only joyful state or blissful state, or a state without confusion. The moment there is choice, it robs you of joy, peace, and quietness.

This world grows with intentions. You build a world in your mind only through your intentions, your own thought process. You go on building a castle, "What are the other people thinking about me?" They are not even thinking about you. You may simply not even exist in another person's consciousness because they are worried about themselves. This is your own world, your own trap that you are caught up in. You need to get out of your own trap. Nothing else can help you. Wake up and realise that this is all just thoughts. Your appreciation of beauty is just a thought, your aversion to an ugly object is just a thought, your craving or aversion is nothing but a passing thought in the mind. Realise this is just a thought and you will be free. Knowing a thought as a thought brings freedom. When you know a thought as a reality that is when you are stuck. Between reality and you, there is thought. Remove this barrier. Then you will appreciate beauty without getting a thought, "Oh, this is beautiful."

Distraction, *vikshepa* and concentration belong to the mind. The Self is beyond tossing and one pointedness. It is the same unchanging pure consciousness at all times. Having known the Self, you don't even need to meditate. You don't need to do anything, you don't need to go into *samadhi*. You can drop everything. Once you are out of the craving, and out of the aversion, you are in to the open field of the self. Then there are no more walls, then you don't need a window, you don't need a door to pass through. Your own concepts have created the wall so you need a door. When there are no concepts, there are no walls then there is no need for any door. You are free. No need to meditate, because meditation belongs to the mind alone. Such mind is blemishless, free of tossing, remains undistorted all the time.

GOING BEYOND REASONS

The world is full of paradoxes and life is full of opposites. The whole art is to embrace the opposites, accommodate the paradoxes and live with a smile. Life is not a simple mathematics, it is a complex mathematics. That's why many things don't appear to be clear to you. So many things don't appear to be clear to so many people, even till the end. They keep asking questions, keep wondering why this, why that, why that... There is no answer for why this, why that. That is how things are. Are you ready to swallow it? Neem is bitter. Why is neem bitter? It is bitter, just swallow it. Mango is sweet, why is mango sweet? You don't know, swallow it. Candy is sweet, why is candy sweet? You don't know, just chew it.

Accommodate the opposites in your life - health and sickness. When you are healthy you never ask the question, "Why am I healthy?" When you fall sick, then you say, "Oh, why am I sick?" Then you try to find all the reasons. No need to connect the reasons unless it's of some use. You can say that you ate some wrong food so you fell sick or you exerted your body too much then you fell sick. It is caused by weather or you caught from somebody else, its' okay. There's no point in analysing it too much. Just see what you need to do.

Too much analysis gets you caught up in your head. Heart transcends reasons. Life transcends reasons. Truth transcends reason. So, someone who is trying to reason out everything all the time can never find truth. Do you see what I'm saying? Why this, why this, why this, why I'm not there, why I'm not here, why I should be this, why I should be that, why that person is like this, why this person is like that. That is how things are. That is it!

Trying to reason out everything puts you in a greater confusion which is unwarranted. Definitely, reason is essential in life, but it has its limitations. It has its perfume; it has its dimension, its area. It should be used only there and not everywhere. Like if you want to measure the temperature in the body, thermometer has to be kept only in certain, particular spots of the body, not everywhere or anywhere. You cannot keep your thermometer on your hair and say okay I have temperature or I don't. So, reason has a place, recognize its place and give it its due place but don't make it enter into all areas of your life. If you just understand this one point, you'll be so free.

This present moment has a mind of its own. The existence has a mind of its own and it knows. And it is running the show. Even now and then if you get reminded of this fact, you'll be at such a peace. You'll be at such ease from your wanting, your craving, that you long for.

Question: Often I meet aggressive people who don't hesitate to hurt others for increasing their power or to get what they want. I would like to handle these situations being in love, but often I get afraid and I also become aggressive. How to handle without behaving like them?
Sri Sri: Smile. See no-one can force you to do, what you don't want to do. So you smile and do what you want to do. (Laughter) You need an act to live in the world. If you think someone is aggressive often

it is your own low self-esteem. Often it's your own feeling of not being attended to. Just examine do you have that feeling within you? Do you want to be given importance? Do you want recognition? Do you want people to be smiling at you all the time?

Okay, you're asking me this question now, whatever answer I give you, at that moment it won't help. Because at that moment you'll forget all these answers. When you are in an aggressive situation if you could just digest and smile and look at that person, why he is aggressive with compassion, your aggression will definitely calm down.

Question: What is the origin of prana?
Sri Sri: When you are thinking of origin you are thinking on a linear dimension. Truth is not linear it is spherical. A sphere has no beginning and no end. Can you tell me, where does a sphere begin? You have a sphere in your hand, where does it begin, where does it end? A sphere does not begin anywhere nor end anywhere. It simply exists. In Sanskrit this is called '*anadi ananta*' beginingless and endless.

Searching for an origin is going on a linear dimension, one line, a single line. If you trace a single line you can go okay, see this is where this line begins. But truth is not that. That's why all these theories of origin of the universe in the world have been failing over and again. Because people have failed, so many theories they have written, volumes and volumes have been written on them and then they have been discarded. In a matter of two decades all these have been discarded. Why? The basic point people forgot. Something need not have a beginning and an end, it can just exist.

Something can exist without a beginning or an end. The ancient *rishis* knew that, that's why they said things are '*anadi ananta*'. They said basically two things one they said the matter, matter never began or ended, they simply change their form. Second is consciousness of the life, life never began nor it ended, it only assumes different forms and transformations happen.

People thought the world is only 50,000 years old and then they thought no it one million years old, it's two million year old and now recently they said its five billion years that planet earth has existed and life has existed, since two billion years. So what happened? All these other theories that man came from ape and monkey and all that, what happened all these theories are on stake. They have all missed this basic truth that at one time everything could exist on this planet simultaneously. It's not one after another. That's why it's said that God has 1000 arms because he could do 1000 things at a time. If he has only two arms then he can only do one after another. First he has to create a monkey and then he has to create a man. If he has a 1000 arms he can do it simultaneously, push them all together on the planet. Just the idea to say that God has 1000 arms means what? Everything has sprung up, has come out at once. Doesn't matter now, we are all here.

Question: You have said that negative emotions have nothing to do with external circumstances but with lack of prana. But let's say if you bear a loss of a loved person, it would be natural for you to get depressed, even if you have plenty of prana. That would imply that external circumstances will have some impact on our feelings, please comment.

Sri Sri: Any external circumstance does have an impact because you are not an isolated island. Even if you are an island, the ocean always touches, connects you, the waves lash on your shores. You are not isolated. You are part of the whole, so definitely if anything happens in your environment, whether to someone who is near and dear to you, or to someone who is just there around you, or even your neighbours, it will definitely affect you. But these effects are short lived. Don't think that will be there forever. No-one can ever be sad to the same degree throughout. In fact you'd be shocked to know that you somehow got the strength and courage to manage all that and moved along.

Life moves ahead. So things will move ahead. Don't try to fight it out. If you are sad, just be sad. Be with that experience for a few minutes or few days, totally. That will give you the realization, see you are also going to be dead. You think you are going to be here permanently? Somebody passed away, you're also going to go there. It's only matter of few years, who knows? We live in this world as though we are never going to die and nobody ever will die. And when someone dies it shocks our system, it wakes us up. Oh is this the truth? Ah, this is the end, is this what's going to happen? Then you will see that all the furniture, all the cars, all the houses, all the money in your banks, and everything will remain here, your body also and you won't be there. Then you are able to laugh more freely, smile. A load is lifted off you.

This is the end. Why do you have to worry. You can use the same situation either you can use it to get depressed or when you wake up and look at it you will move in knowledge, you'll move in awareness, you'll become much brilliant, both in your heart and in your head.

FOUR TRICKS TO SAVE YOUR MIND

When we talk, we listen and we understand differently. When we hear a talk, everyone understands it differently. But when a sound is uttered or sung, the same sound resonates in all the minds. So on one level one sound unites everybody. Everyone smiles, right? And also our right brain activity which is music becomes alive. Both sides of the brain, logic and music have to be balanced. *Yoga* means bringing balance. So in *yoga* this is called '*nada yoga*', the *yoga* of sound, music. Singing is essential, and in singing the Sanskrit chants, the *mantras* have an added advantage. *Mantras* are very potent sounds, the meaning is not important, just the sound itself is important. These *maha mantras* energize the consciousness, reverberates the depth of the consciousness, so they were called *Mantras*. *Mantra* means that which helps the mind to unite with the spirit, that which helps the mind to energize itself. While doing activities the mental energy goes out. We are spending a lot of mental energy. You are looking, it's the mind that's looking through the eyes absorbing the information, the same way hearing, smelling, touching, the whole process of perception happens through mind and every time you perceive, you are tiring yourself, you are draining your energy. It's natural, you can't avoid it. How to recuperate this energy? It is by chanting these *Mantras*.

The ancient sounds are obviously in Sanskrit and Latin, the oldest languages. If you go on the expedition of knowledge how different languages developed, they go to Indo-Germanic ie: Sanskrit, German and Latin. These are the two main languages. Now the added advantage of Sanskrit is that it is so co-related with the nature; the sound, the object, and its function are co-related. For example - anywhere in the world what do you say when you want people to be silent? (Shhhhhh) If you say this, everybody becomes silent and what's sound that comes out when you are astonished? Wow! If you are so astonished by the power of silence what is the sound that would come? 'Shhhh and wow' is *Shiva*. *Shiva* means the inner most silence, that wow state. When people had gone deep in meditation what they found? That's the depth of consciousness, the stillness, the silence where they united with the entire cosmos (wow) '*Shiva*'.

In the same way the word nervous system in English comes from the word '*nara*' meaning the nervous system. '*Nara*' is a Sanskrit word. The human beings are called '*Naras*' because they have the highly developed nervous system. If you speak English, you look closely, there are a lot of Sanskrit words in it. 70% of the English language has Sanskrit. '*Duhita*' in Sanskrit is 'daughter' in English, '*swasa*' is 'sister', '*suta*' is 'son', '*maata*' is 'mother'. In the same way you can go on, if you go on and on you will find about 70% of the language contains Sanskrit words.

The original Sanskrit words, *Mantras*, are very powerful in the sense our consciousness is very old and the deepest layer of our consciousness also resonates with that sound. Now if we sing 'Aleluya', it's not English but Latin. If you go deeper into Latin roots, you will find that there is one sound that unifies. So, that is one added advantage of singing the *mantras*, they reverberate and energize the whole system. *Mantras* are also a part of the philosophy of *yoga*. Similarly 'OM', when you say 'aa' the effect is like of the 1st stage *pranayama*, when you say 'uu', it's the middle and when you say 'mm' it's the 3rd stage *pranayama*. So, when you chant 'Om' all the three *'pranayamas'* are happening. The life force is moving up. Similarly when you say *'Hari'*, the *'ha'* *pranayama* resonates the lower portion and the *'ri'* *pranayama* top of the head. *'Hari'*, the *prana* is made to rise up. 'Hari' means all the pain vanishes and the *prana* moves up. So, the sounds do make an impact on the system, though it's very subtle. But it doesn't matter, you can sing any song in any language and that's still a part of *Satsang* because your right brain becomes active. The added advantage of these few sounds are that they unite vertically deep inside your consciousness also. So, when *mantras* are chanted or sung the meanings are not important, just the vibrations.

Question: How to deal with a selfish or weird person?
Sri Sri: I think we should think of many ways and all the ways are through 'Love'. Handle a selfish person with love. Try to understand why they are selfish. They have not experienced love in their lives so they become selfish. They don't trust others so they have become selfish. Give them more love, create a sense of belongingness with them. Even a Gorilla has a family, a dacoit though he maybe a violent man for everyone else but he has someone very close to him, at least

with them he has human values. I don't see a single human being who is bad totally, 100%. They have one or two percent goodness in them. Pick up that goodness and make them grow from that. Make that goodness in that person grow. This is very important and don't brand them as bad. It's the circumstances that make them behave in that way. So, I always feel there is a hope for the weirdest person to become the most normal and loving person in the society. So, keep the hope.

The propounder of *yoga 'Maharshi Patanjali'* has given four *sutras* ie: four tricks, methods, formulas or techniques on how to save your own mind. Save your mind by having four attitudes.

There are four types of people on this planet. One is who are happy. You will be friendly with people who are happy. Have friendship with the people who are happy because if you are not friendly with people who are happy and prosperous, you will give rise to jealousy within yourself. You will have hatred for them and you will try to find fault in them. These qualities, these imperfections in the mind will start coming up. So when you find someone happy, what should you do? Shake hands, be friendly with them, know that they are you friends. When your friends are happy, will you be upset? No. You will say my friend is happy and so I am happy and if your friend is unhappy, you will also become unhappy. So, be friendly with those who are happy.

What about those who are miserable? Don't be friendly with the miserable ones, 90% of the times a person becomes miserable due to his own mind, his own doings. So, what to do with people who are miserable? Be compassionate. There is difference between being friendly and being compassionate. If you are friendly, your vision will also get blurred and you too will go in the same direction. If a friend is miserable and he is angry at somebody, and if you go and shake hands with him you will also become angry and miserable, instead have compassion for those who are miserable. Circumstances has made them miserable, help them out. You can't be compassionate with a happy person. How can you be compassionate with a happy person? You can only be compassionate only when someone is miserable. So, develop the quality of compassion within you when you look at miserable people. This is a way of bringing out compassion within you. Be compassionate with people who are miserable.

When someone is doing good work be happy for them. And if someone is doing horrible work what to do? You've to save your mind, be indifferent to them, don't hate them. You know if we start hating, our mind gets on to the same boat. That man hates something and you start hating him and you're no better. You both hate different objects, that's all. Your object of hatred is different but you become hateful. So, save your mind from hatred and for that be indifferent. Our attitude should be of indifference towards people who are doing wrong things but not our action. You act to correct them but inside you, you have an indifferent attitude. Only when you have indifference you will be able give proper judgment or teach.

Suppose what some person is doing is harmful and if you tell them what you are doing is harmful to me, don't do it, he won't stop. If you tell him what you are doing is going to cause harm to you my dear, don't do it, then you are teacher to that person. You are able to educate them, he will understand. Your behaviour is not good for you is the way to make someone aware of his mistake rather than saying your behaviour is not good for me, stop doing it for my sake. No one will do it.

Maharshi Patanjali told this in the ancient times - how to save your mind, with friendliness, compassion, happiness and indifference. Keep these four attitudes in your heart, you don't have to practice it. You simply have to assume they are within your. Keep it in your heart and it will automatically manifest. It will spontaneously happen in your life. What will be the result of doing this? Your mind will be in pleasant state, your mind will have peace, grace will flow in your mind and when it flows in your mind, it will flow through you to everybody.

Qustion: How can I avoid stress?
Sri Sri: Don't try to avoid stress, don't be scared about it. If it comes, okay, let it come. If you are so scared of stress then you get stressed even more.

When you are bicycling for the first time, if you are so worried that you'd hit a stone, you are definitely going to hit a stone or the pavement. Stress is there. Okay, let it come, so what? It's a part of life. Sometimes you get stressed and sometimes you become happy, so what? Take them all and move on. Don't sit back and brood over the past or find fault in others. We should drop all this. What do you say? Right? At home you have a dustbin, right? You put all the garbage into it. Suppose there is no garbage bin at your home, the garbage will be all over. So, it's good to have a place and put it there and accept it. In the same way let some stress come or imperfection come once in a while in the life. Okay, so what, let it be there. Let's move on and not poke our nose into the garbage can. Definitely keep it somewhere in the home but don't sleep on it.

Qustion: The family business is the source of permanent stress, extreme effort and hard work, what should I do?
Sri Sri: You know, there is no job devoid of stress. Either you have the stress of your own or you have the stress of everybody else or the world. It is the attitude of the mind if it wants to take it as a stress, anything can be stressful but if you have that confidence, if you know the best will happen to you, your mind is clear, your heart is clear. In business there is always ups and downs, it will come and go. Don't do your business emotionally, do it with intellect and don't do charity with intellect, do it with your heart. Service with heart and business with head and bringing the balance between these two is wisdom. I understand that it's not easy for a person of heart to do business. It's not easy when you just flow emotionally but you

have to practice that. Charity cannot happen from an empty bowl. You should have some substance so that you can give. If your bowl is empty, what can you give? Right? But when there is trust in the divinity, trust in the laws of universe then you don't have to worry about anything. Everything will happen spontaneously. Okay!

The Art of Living
&
The International Association for Human Values

Transforming Lives

The Founder

His Holiness Sri Sri Ravi Shankar

His Holiness Sri Sri Ravi Shankar is a universally revered spiritual and humanitarian leader. His vision of a violence-free, stress-free society through the reawakening of human values has inspired millions to broaden their spheres of responsibility and work towards the betterment of the world. Born in 1956 in southern India, Sri Sri was often found deep in meditation as a child. At the age of four, astonishes his teachers by reciting the Bhagavad Gita, an ancient Sanskrit scripture. He has always had the unique gift of presenting the deepest truths in the simplest of words.

Sri Sri established the Art of Living, an educational and humanitarian Non-Governmental Organisation that works in special consultative status with the Economic and Social Council (ECOSOC) of the United Nations in 1981. Present in over 151 countries, it formulates and implements lasting solutions to conflicts and issues faced by individuals, communities and nations. In 1997, he founded the International Association for Human Values (IAHV) to foster human values and lead sustainable development projects. Sri Sri has reached out to an estimated 300 million people worldwide through personal interactions, public events, teachings,

Art of Living workshops and humanitarian initiatives. He has brought to the masses ancient practices which were traditionally kept exclusive, and has designed many self development techniques which can easily be integrated into daily life to calm the mind and instil confidence and enthusiasm. One of Sri Sri's most unique offerings to the world is the Sudarshan Kriya, a powerful breathing technique that facilitates physical, mental, emotional and social well-being.

Numerous honours have been bestowed upon Sri Sri, including the Order of the Pole Star (the highest state honour in Mongolia), the Peter the Great Award (Russian Federation), the Sant Shri Dnyaneshwara World Peace Prize (India) and the Global Humanitarian Award (USA). Sri Sri has addressed several international forums, including the United Nations Millennium World Peace Summit (2000), the World Economic Forum (2001, 2003) and several parliaments across the globe.

The Art of Living
In Service Around The World

(www.artofliving.org)

The largest volunteer-based network in the world, with a wide range of social, cultural and spiritual activities, the Art of Living has reached out to over 20 million people from all walks of life, since 1982. A non-profit, educational, humanitarian organization, it is committed to creating peace from the level of the individual upwards, and fostering human values within the global community. Currently, the Art of Living service projects and educational programmes are carried out in over 151 countries. The organisation works in special consultative status with the Economic and Social Council (ECOSOC) of the United Nations, participating in a variety of committees and activities related to health and conflict resolution.

The Art of Living
Stress Elimination Programmes

Holistic Development of Body, Mind & Spirit The Art of Living programmes are a combination of the best of ancient wisdom and modern science. They cater to every age group - children, youth, adults -and every section of society – rural communities, governments, corporate houses, etc. Emphasizing holistic living and personal self-development, the programmes facilitate the complete blossoming of an individual's full potential. The cornerstone of all our workshops is the Sudarshan Kriya, a unique, potent breathing practice.

• The Art of Living Course Part I
• The Art of Living Course Part II
• Sahaj Samadhi Meditation
• Divya Samaaj ka Nirmaan (DSN)
• The All Round Training in Excellence (ART Excel)
• The Youth Empowerment Seminar (YES) (for 15-18 year olds)
• The Youth Empowerment Seminar Plus (YES+) (for 18+ year olds)
• The Prison Programme
• Achieving Personal Excellence Program (APEX) www.apexprogram.org
• Sri Sri Yoga www.srisriyoga.in

The International Association
for Human Values
(www.iahv.org)

The International Association for Human Values (IAHV) was founded in Geneva in 1997, to foster, on a global scale, a deeper understanding of the values that unite us as a single human community. Its vision is to celebrate distinct traditions and diversity, while simultaneously creating a greater understanding and appreciation of our many shared principles. To this end, the IAHV develops and promotes programmes that generate awareness and encourage the practice of human values in everyday life. It upholds that the incorporation of human values into all aspects of life, will ultimately lead to harmony amidst diversity, and the development of a more peaceful, just and sustainable world. The IAHV works in collaboration with partners dedicated to similar goals, including governments, multilateral agencies, educational institutions, NGOs, corporations and individuals.

Service Projects
• Sustainable Rural Development
• Organic Farming
• Trauma Relief
• Peace Initiatives
• Education (www.ssrvm.org)
• Women Empowerment
• Drug Addiction Rehabilitation

International Centres

INDIA
21st KM, Kanakapura Road Udayapura
Bangalore – 560 082
Karnataka
Telephone : +91-80-28427060
Fax : +91-80-28432832
Email : info@vvmvp.org
CANADA
13 Infinity Road
St. Mathieu du Parc
Quebec G0x 1n0
Telephone : +819- 532-3328
Fax : +819-532-2033
Email : artdevivre@artofliving.org
GERMANY
Bad Antogast 1
D - 77728 Oppenau.
Telephone : +49 7804-910 923
Fax : +49 7804-910 924
Email : artofliving.germany@t-online.de

www.srisriravishankar.org
www.artofliving.org
www.iahv.org
www.5h.org